THE *fruitful* SEASON

Prayers for the autumn of life

By Catherine Whiteman
Illustrated by David Whiteman

Mary,
God bless you with peace,
love & joy —
Catherine Whiteman

Beaver's Pond Press, Inc.

Edina, Minnesota

ISBN 10: 1-59298-186-0
ISBN 13: 978-1-59298-186-1

Library of Congress Control Number: 2007924463
Printed in the United States of America
First Printing: May 2007
11   10   09   08   07   6   5   4   3   2   1

Illustrations and design by David Whiteman

All biblical passages come from the Revised Standard Version of the Holman Study Bible.

Beaver's Pond Press, Inc.
7104 Ohms Lane, Suite 216
Edina, MN 55439-2129
(952) 829-8818
www.BeaversPondPress.com
Beaver's Pond Press is an imprint of Beaver's Pond Group.

To order, visit www.BookHouseFulfillment.com
or call 1-800-901-3480. Reseller discounts available.

Dedication

To my family and friends,
who have provided so much support
and encouragement.

Thank you! I love you.

Christmas 2007

A Gift For:

Mary King

From:

Gabriel J. Phillips

+FYI... The author, Cathy, is Diane's (Christopher's Godmother)
sister. Enjoy!!

The smaller your physical sphere becomes, the more influence you have in the spiritual realm, which is eternal. Do not fear aging or physical limits. If your ear is tuned to the still, small whisper of God's voice, periods of crisis, illness or old age become the most fruitful seasons of life.

Acknowledgements

This little book began as a thought several years ago. If it had not been for the talent and generosity of my son Dave, thus it would have remained. His beautiful photography and talent as a computer artist gave life to this idea. The time we spent together taking pictures and creating a format for this book will always be among the most precious experiences of my life. We truly come to the fruitful season when our adult children give us the gift of themselves.

I want to cover the earth with color ...

I want to grow fields of yellow daisies and buttercups ...

I want the moon to cast a soft glow, eliminating the shadows that cause fear among us ...

I would like the voice of winter to whisper only words of encouragement ...

"Spring comes. Spring comes."

If each of us listens to the voice of the Spirit and creates a small thing of beauty, we will have the power to change our world. Heaven will be made manifest upon the earth. I pray this small book will assist you to let God's Holy Spirit flow through your life.

Cathy Whiteman

A prayer

of praise

Holy Spirit, help me to pray.

Holy God, I praise you. You are worthy of constant praise and thanksgiving, you who create all beauty, truth, grace, and love. You are able. You are gracious and full of mercy. You are kind. You are love! Praise you. It is difficult for me to find the words to praise you because you are so beyond my imagining. However, I can praise you for your goodness and faithfulness, for I have experienced these. You have been so faithful to me as I've gone through life's challenges. You have given me hope and strength when I had none. I thank you, Father, for your kindness and graciousness toward me. Praise you forever. I look forward to praising you in heaven when I have more ways to describe your greatness. Alleluia!

Amen.

Praise the Lord!

Praise God in his sanctuary; praise him in his mighty firmament! Praise him for his mighty deeds; praise him according to his exceeding greatness!

Praise him with trumpet sound; praise him with lute and harp! Praise him with timbrel and dance; praise him with strings and pipe! Praise him with sounding cymbals; praise him with loud clashing cymbals! Let everything that breathes praise the Lord! Praise the Lord!

Psalms 150:1–6

A prayer for love

Spirit of All, I seek to learn your lessons of love. I confess that I have no strength of my own, no knowledge of my own, no ability of my own. My body is getting older and my mind is less clear than it used to be. I often feel empty. Yet I want to stop striving: striving to look good, striving to accomplish things, striving to control the things and people around me. I want to simply rest in the fact that I am your child. You love me, even when I do nothing. I do not need to earn your love. I do not need to pretend that I am more than I am. My mind wants to rest, to be fully present in the moment rather than race ahead with anxiety and fear. Help me to trust that, whatever and wherever life brings me, I will never be beyond you and your care for me, no matter what. Help me to share the love of Jesus Christ with people in my life. Praise you, my creator, I love you. Help me to do your will. Help me to remember who I am, that I only have to do what you've given me to do, and that your love helps me to do what you've asked of me.

Amen.

The law of the Lord is perfect, reviving the soul; the testimony of the Lord is sure, making wise the simple; the precepts of the Lord are right; rejoicing the heart; the commandment of the Lord is pure, enlightening the eyes; the fear of the Lord is clean, enduring forever; the ordinances of the Lord are true, and righteous altogether. More to be desired are they than gold, even much fine gold; sweeter also than honey and drippings of the honeycomb.

Psalms 19:7–10

A prayer to the Holy Spirit

May the Holy Spirit constantly fill us. May we remain open in the midst of all our activities, always aware of the gentle whispering of the eternal God. I know I must not speak as much as listen. I must not get so busy as to forget who is giving me the strength and breath for the task at hand. I must never get too self-important that I fail to take the time to listen carefully to each person. Help me, Holy Spirit, for these things do not come easily to a mortal person. I struggle with myself, always trying to get past self-absorption. You are the reward of my seeking. I constantly seek you and you reveal yourself to me through the love of people, through the beauty of nature, through music, through the voice that speaks softly saying, "Do not be afraid of life." Thank you, Holy Spirit!

Amen.

When the Spirit of truth comes, he will guide you into all the truth; for he will not speak on his own authority, but whatever he hears he will speak, and he will declare to you the things that are to come.

John 16:13

A prayer of
Thanksgiving

Heavenly Father, the spring speaks to me of you. The green is deep and rich. The air is heavy with the fragrance of blossoms and it is gentle and soft. The winter has been so harsh. Now the gentle spring is here. Thank you, Father, that you bless us, all of us, not just those who serve you. You give the gift of spring even to those who deny you. I thank you.

I love you. I am weak. I am tired, but this small person loves you. I pray you can accept the gift of this love and somehow add it to all that is beautiful.

Amen.

You have heard that it was said, "You shall love your neighbor and hate your enemy." But I say to you, love your enemies and pray for those who persecute you, so that you may be sons of your Father who is in heaven; for he makes his sun rise on the evil and on the good, and sends rain on the just and on the unjust. For if you love those who love you, what reward have you?

Matthew 5:43–46

A prayer for renewal

Mighty God, before I turn to my work again, I must take time to turn to you. I seek beauty, harmony, and health. Thank you for the beautiful resurrection of your son, Jesus Christ. The quiet lessons of nature, as spring returns, speak to us saying, "You and I can make all things new again." I want to share the love of Jesus. I want to be able to speak of Him. How can I do this? How shall I walk? Where should I go? I do not want my ego to get in the way of sharing you with others. Please renew me and show me the way. Help me to respect the paths of faith that others walk. Help me to have humility. Help me to love even those who do not love me or who seem to be at odds with me. Help me to see the beauty in each person. When pain or fear threaten to destroy our peace, may we turn to you and be renewed.

Praise you! Alleluia!

Amen.

As a doe longs for flowing streams, so longs my soul for thee, O God. My soul thirsts for God, for the living God. When shall I come and behold the face of God?

Psalms 42:1–2

One thing I asked of the Lord, that will I seek after; that I may dwell in the house of the Lord all the days of my life, to behold the beauty of the Lord, and to inquire in His temple. ... Wait for the Lord; be strong, and let your heart take courage; yea, wait for the Lord.

Psalms 27:4,14

A prayer
for generosity

Loving God, I know that my life is a gift; it is not mine to hang on to. My children are a gift. They are not mine, but a gift of joy to cherish. I must not hang on to them. My friends, my job, my home…all are lent to me for a season. Your Word stresses generosity of giving and of loving. So that I can generously let go, help me to know that you will provide abundantly for every good thing. You, God, love a cheerful giver! Alleluia!

Amen.

Light rises in the darkness for the upright; the Lord is gracious, merciful and righteous. It is well with the man who deals generously and lends, who conducts his affairs with justice, for the righteous will never be moved; he will be remembered forever. He is not afraid of evil tidings; his heart is firm, trusting in the Lord. His heart is steady, he will not be afraid, until he sees his desire on his adversaries. He has distributed freely, he has given to the poor; his righteousness endures forever ...

Psalms 112:4–9

A prayer
for healing

Lord, there is no one I can talk with about this except you. No one cares as much as you do or understands me as well. I am ill. I am exhausted. I bring it on myself; no one else inflicts it upon me. I try to do too much for people rather than allow them to do for themselves. I do not love myself in a healthy way. Jesus took the time away from ministry for prayer and rest. Help me, Lord, to pattern myself after Jesus. I want to share Him with others, especially my family. I don't know how to do it without turning people away. Show me, Holy Spirit. I would like to be able to say to people, "Jesus is the way."

Alleluia, alleluia, I love you, Father. Thank you for all you have given me. I pray for all people suffering loss, pain, or exhaustion. Restore unto us the joy of your salvation and uphold us with your mercy.

Amen.

Draw near to God and he will draw near to you.

James 4:8

Bless the Lord, O my soul; and all that is within, bless his holy name. Bless the Lord, O my soul, and forget not all his benefits, who forgives all your iniquity, who heals all your diseases, who redeems your life from the pit, who crowns you with steadfast love and mercy, who satisfies you with good as long as you live so that your youth is renewed like the eagle's.

Psalms 103:1–5

A prayer
for humility

It is difficult for me to pray right now, God. I feel compelled to be working every minute of the day. I know compulsion does not flow from your Holy Spirit, so I ask your help to listen to the Spirit and not compulsion. Help me to lay aside my ego and my need to be important. Help me to be your servant and do your will; use me for your honor and glory. I must learn to keep my good deeds quiet. Only in this way can you use me in the way you would like. Sometimes I serve you best in silence and inactivity. Holy Spirit, help me not to forget this.

Amen.

The point is this; he who sows sparingly will also reap sparingly, and he who sows bountifully will also reap bountifully. Each one must do as he has made up his mind, not reluctantly or under compulsion, for God loves a cheerful giver. And God is able to provide you with every blessing in abundance, so that you may always have enough of everything and may provide in abundance for every good work.

2 Corinthians 9:6–8

A prayer

for courage

Lord, I come to you this morning, opening the door of my heart. Help me not to fear, for my fear is not from you, but only from a lack of trust and love. Help me to know you are in control. I want to have time to worship you, to make music, to make a home, to have time for family and friends. I know in order to do this, I must let go of all I have worked so hard to gain—financial security—which is no security at all. And this takes courage I don't always have. Help me to take the gifts that you offer at each moment. Help me today to make wise decisions about the use of my time. Help me to treat each person I meet today with love and respect. I seek to serve you. Alleluia!

Amen.

Even the sparrow finds a home, and the swallow a nest for herself, where she may lay her young ...

Psalms 84:3

For a day in Your court is better than a thousand elsewhere ... For the Lord God is a sun and shield; he bestows favor and honor. No good thing does the Lord withhold from those who walk uprightly. O Lord of hosts, blessed is the man who trusts in thee!

Psalms 84:10–12

A prayer
for victory

In the name of Jesus Christ, I claim the promise that Satan has no power over me. He constantly tries to defeat me, but when I turn to Jesus, Satan must flee. Again today, I claim the promise and rejoice that I am safe. When I was a child, I knew God loved me. I hope all children, especially children abandoned, children abused, children wounded by divorce, children who are hungry, children who live in the midst of war, know God is there. I lift them up to you and ask you to reveal yourself to them.

"We would see Jesus." Do those who search see Jesus in me? I would decrease so He may increase. I lift up our hurting world. I pray for peace and prosperity for all people. I pray that love will prevail over evil and hate. I pray for beauty to grow and ugliness to decrease. I pray that heaven will come down to earth. Alleluia!

Amen.

But thanks be to God, who gives us the victory through our Lord Jesus Christ. Therefore, my beloved brethren, be steadfast, immovable, always abounding in the work of the Lord, knowing that in the Lord your labor is not in vain.

I Corinthians 15:57–58

A prayer
for guidance

Lord, I come to you this morning and ask for your guidance, that your hand will guide me daily. Praise you, Creator God, for the beautiful gift of this day. Thank you for the warmth of the sun, the gentleness of the breeze and the colors that are so evident; the green of the grass, the many colored flowers and birds, the blue skies and beautiful pinks of the evening. Thank you. Surely a lifetime is like a breath in terms of eternity. Help me to share the love of Jesus every day and not to be afraid to share what He has done for me. Help me now to prioritize the jobs that need to be done today. May I listen for your voice and be open to your will being done through me. Alleluia!

Amen!

If you pour yourself out for the hungry and satisfy the desire of the afflicted, then shall your light rise in the darkness and your gloom be as the noonday. And the Lord will guide you continually, and satisfy your desire with good things, and make your bones strong; and you shall be like a watered garden, like a spring of water, whose waters fail not.

Isaiah 59:10–11

My soul magnifies the Lord, and my spirit rejoices in God my Savior.

Luke 1:46–47

A prayer

for hope

Spirit of Life, thank you for bringing me through another night of rest into a beautiful day. It is my favorite time of year, when the days are cool and crisp and there is change in the air. I anticipate the turning of the leaves, but there is a sadness, too, as the flowers lose their brightness and their beauty. The comfort lies in knowing that next spring, you and I together can bring back the beauty of the flowers by nurturing new seeds, seeds that came from this year's flowers. Color will return again. Help me to remember this lesson. I have had the bloom of my life. Now it is time to plant new seeds, to nurture and encourage beauty in the next generation. I know that my "color" has not faded completely, but I feel it beginning to fade. I will not be sad, but count this time of my life as the best. I will be less concerned about myself and more able to help others. What a glorious thought. Help me to nurture my children and other people's children. Alleluia!

Amen.

For Thou, O Lord, art my hope, my trust, O Lord, from my youth. Upon thee I have leaned from my birth; thou art he who took me from my mother's womb. My praise is continually of thee. Do not cast me off in the time of old age; forsake me not when my strength is spent.

Psalms 71:5–6,9

My mouth will tell of thy righteous acts of thy deeds of salvation all the day, for their number is past my knowledge. O God, from my youth thou has taught me, and I still proclaim thy wondrous deeds. So even to old age and gray hairs, O God, do not forsake me, till I proclaim thy might to all the generations to come...

Psalms 71:15,17–18

A prayer for trust

Merciful God, I have lost my way. I feel baffled and confused. All my life, ever since I can remember, I have sought you and listened for your guidance, but if I cannot trust the internal voice that guides my decisions, where do I turn? Why would your voice encourage me to follow my dream, a dream that then shatters? I know you are a loving creator, and do not wish pain or failure to be the result of following prayerfully sought guiding lights. I just somehow need to know I can trust the voice that I have always believed was yours. Have I fooled myself and only listened to my own ego? This cannot be, because often the voice leads me away from myself. I think I tried to put you in a box, to know everything was going to work out effortlessly because it was your will. Then I was disappointed when it did not work out at all. Do you hear me, Father God? I know people have faced more crushing blows than I have and have had dreams shattered by death and disease. I am sure people have crises of faith when their very lives are being taken from them. Please, do not abandon me, even in my lesser trials.

Amen.

Do not feel sorry for yourself.

Love and care for others.

Have fun.

Have renewed interest in making things beautiful.

Give yourself fully to your work.

Stay involved.

Take risks.

Take care of yourself.

Truly, truly I say to you, unless a grain of wheat falls into the earth and dies, it remains alone; but if it dies, it bears much fruit. He who loves his life loses it, and he who hates his life in this world will keep it for eternal life. If any one serves me, he must follow me; and where I am, there shall my servant be also; if any one serves me, the Father will honor him.

John 12:24–26

A prayer
for charity

Lord, I am struggling with my selfishness. I ask you to give me the power of the Holy Spirit to choose loving actions and words. I know I have failed again and I ask your forgiveness. I love you, God. I believe you listen and honor my prayers in profound ways that are beyond my understanding. It comforts me to know that you love me and want good things for me. Thank you for giving me life. May I constantly use the gift of a listening ear to hear your voice and not depend upon my own limited resources. This way I can serve others! Come into me today, Lord, and use my body, my voice, my talents for your purposes. Help me to delight in the graces and veil the defects of those I love. I pray in the name of Jesus, who showed us the way.

Thank you, Jesus.

Amen.

If anyone says, "I love God," and hates his brother, he is a liar; for he who does not love his brother whom he has seen, cannot love God whom he has not seen.

I John 4:20

Love is patient and kind; love is not jealous or boastful; it is not arrogant or rude. Love does not insist on its own way; it is not irritable or resentful; it does not rejoice at wrong, but rejoices in the right. Love bears all things, believes all things, hopes all things, endures all things.

I Corinthians 13:4–7

A prayer
for direction

Father God, I come to you before I return to my duties and responsibilities. I long to hear your voice, but my cares and concerns drown out your still, small voice. Help me to put aside my fears, longings, and passions and to listen for you. I long to do your will. Show me the direction you would have me go. Please show me the way to love people as Christ does; show me how to share Him with others. Help me not to be afraid to speak of Jesus as the answer to our longings.

Spirit of the Living God, I know you are there and I know you love me. I hear your voice often say to me, "I love you. I want to bless you richly. Do not be afraid of anything. Your children will be your blessing. Trust me in all things." I know these words come from you who made me. I want to abandon myself completely to those words and live in peace, but my humanness and sin get in the way. Help me to go beyond my fears and enter into the dance of life.

I pray for all who are suffering and sad today. Lift them up and turn them toward you. Alleluia!

Amen.

Commit your way to the Lord; trust in him and he will act!

Psalms 37:5

A prayer for strength

Dear God, author of life, creator of all that is, sustainer of life: you are mystery. You are: I know you are. You love me and want to bless me. Even in my moments of despair and deep disappointment, you want to bless me. I love you, God. I confess that I am simply a person with limited strength. Hope, though, lies in what Jesus taught us: it is when we are weak that we are strong. I pray you will demonstrate your strength through my life. Complete reliance upon you will produce perfect peace, and fear will have no power over me. Thanks be to God!

Amen.

In thee, O Lord, do I seek refuge: let me never be put to shame; in thy righteousness deliver me! Incline thy ear to me, rescue me speedily! Be thou a rock of refuge for me, a strong fortress to save me! Yea, thou art my rock and my fortress; for thy name's sake lead me and guide me, take me out of the net which is hidden for me, for thou art my refuge. Into thy hand I commit my spirit; thou hast redeemed me, O Lord, faithful God.

Psalms 31:1–5

Be gracious to me, O Lord, for I am in distress.

Psalms 31:9

Be strong and let your heart take courage, all you who wait for the Lord!

Psalms 31:24

A prayer
for awareness

Merciful God, we should be aware of our sins, particularly during Lent. When I think of my sin, Lord, I think of weakness, of all the things I cannot or choose not to do in your name. My weariness makes me long for rest and quiet time with you, but I don't always seek you. I do not intentionally turn from you, but my desire to be recognized gets in the way of doing your good work. My ego, my selfishness; therein lies my sin. Help me to overcome my need to be needed. Help me to listen to you, to act upon your guidance and your words. Thank you for my life. Help me to treat my body gently and provide it opportunities for rest. Help me to keep a prayerful attitude. You have instructed us to love you, to love ourselves, and to love others. Help me, O Lord, to do your will. Alleluia! Praise you, merciful God.

I love you.

Amen.

For I know my transgressions, my sins are always before me.

A prayer
for clarity

I have wondered, God, who can I share my struggles with? Who can listen to my problems and guide me? I think of friends and family members, but would they understand? I know that I can come to you freely and openly with my struggles and you faithfully show me the way. If I would keep you at the forefront, I would not get lost. At least I know that I am simply a creature and you are the creator. Help me, Lord, to trust life and be open to its possibilities. In the name of Jesus Christ who was and is the God of love.

Amen.

... It seemed to me a wearisome task, until I went into the sanctuary of God ...

Psalms 73:16–17

But for me it is good to be near God; I have made the Lord God my refuge, that I may tell of all thy works.

Psalms 73:28

A prayer for joy

I seek you, Spirit of God. I am languishing. I am weary. Help me to love myself enough to take care of my body and my spirit. I pray that people will learn to live in love and peace. I pray for an end to racial hatred. I pray for an end to the slaughter of innocents. I pray for a respectful and loving end to life for all people. I pray you would show me the way to do your work here on earth. I am weak. I am a sinner. I rarely get by my ego, but I want to serve you and I know you can use someone like me. You used Peter and he was a sinner, too. I ask you to help me listen and follow. Help me to make things beautiful wherever and whenever I can. Bless us, Lord, for we are weak. Do not leave us to our own devices. Do not abandon us. When we are left on our own, we are capable of terrible things. Please help us, O Lord. Jesus be our guide and comfort, helping us to create beauty and joy.

Amen.

... I have loved you with an everlasting love; therefore I have continued my faithfulness to you.

Jeremiah 31:3

... I will make them walk by brooks of water, in a straight path in which they shall not stumble.

Jeremiah 31:9

... Keep your voice from weeping, and your eyes from tears; for your work shall be rewarded, says the Lord, and they shall come back from the land of the enemy. There is hope for your future, says the Lord.

Jeremiah 31:16–17

... Set up way marks for yourself, make yourself guideposts; consider well the highway, the road by which you went.

Jeremiah 31:21

For I will satisfy the weary soul, and every languishing soul, I will replenish. ... I will put my law within them, and I will write it upon their hearts; and I will be their God, and they shall be my people.

Jeremiah 31:25,33

notes

notes

notes